Vietnam Junkyard
and Other Poems

VOLUMES:

1. FIRST REFLECTIONS
2. VIETNAM JUNKYARD
3. MILLENNIAL MEDITATIONS

Vietnam Junkyard and Other Poems

(1998-2006)

Ed Calhoon

COPYRIGHT © 2008 BY ED CALHOON.

Front Cover Photo: U.S. Army Photograph, August, 1991. CW3 Ed Calhoon USAR (ret.) (right) was awarded the Meritorious Service Medal during the monthly retirement parade at Fort George G. Meade, MD. Also honored was CW4 Ed Green (left). CW4 Green was the Supply Officer of the U.S. Army Field Band in his final assignment, and previously commanded the First Army Band. CW3 Calhoon was an enlisted tuba player in both the First Army Band and Army Field Band in 1961-1963. Prior to the retirement ceremony, CW4 Green conducted the First Army Band and CW3 Calhoon played a sousaphone with the band.

LIBRARY OF CONGRESS CONTROL NUMBER: 2007908641
ISBN: HARDCOVER 978-1-4363-0061-2
SOFTCOVER 978-1-4363-0060-5

All rights reserved. No part of this book may be reproduced or transmitted in any form or by any means, electronic or mechanical, including photocopying, recording, or by any information storage and retrieval system, without permission in writing from the copyright owner.

This book was printed in the United States of America.

To order additional copies of this book, contact:
Xlibris Corporation
1-888-795-4274
www.Xlibris.com
Orders@Xlibris.com
44670

CONTENTS

VOLUME 1
FIRST REFLECTIONS

- MEMORIES ... 1-1
  - Pre-Boomer Nostalgia ... 1-3
  - Ham Radio History ... 1-7
  - Summer of 59 ... 1-10
  - High Hopes Realized ... 1-13
- FAMILY ... 1-17
  - Our father ... 1-19
  - Four Generations of Grandfathers, Fathers and Sons ... 1-21
  - Sonnet on Mother's Dying ... 1-28
  - Kate ... 1-29
- ANIMALS ... 1-31
  - Two Tom Cats ... 1-33
  - Two Royal Felines ... 1-35
  - Geoffrey the Poodle ... 1-37
- PLACES ... 1-39
  - City of Angels ... 1-41
  - Sunset Beach ... 1-43
  - Country Church Strawberry Festival ... 1-45
  - Why do I live in Arnold, Maryland? ... 1-47
- DISEASES ... 1-49
  - Mother's Schizoid Rant ... 1-51
  - Dad's Alzheimer's ... 1-53
  - Shared Surgery ... 1-56
  - My Parkinson's ... 1-57
  - Cancer Survivor ... 1-60
- FUN ... 1-63
  - To The Tuba—Cinquain So Low ... 1-65
  - A Tubist's Haiku ... 1-66
  - Haiku on Writing ... 1-67

Volume 2
Vietnam Junkyard

1. Vietnam Volunteer 2-1
2. Flight to Nam 2-8
3. Cam Ranh Bay 2-12
4. Keystone Battalion 2-16
5. Da Nang Junkyard 2-23
6. Wash Rack Crew 2-34
7. Inspections (Haircuts, Uniforms and Drugs) 2-38
8. Fraggings 2-43
9. Plain Clothes Police 2-45
10. Problems with alcohol 2-48
11. Evacuation Hospital 2-51
12. Chapel 2-53
13. Feeling Unappreciated 2-56
14. Ammo Officer 2-60
15. Return to the world 2-66
16. Be All You Can Be In the Army Reserve 2-68
17. Call Me Mister Ed 2-70
18. Fading Away 2-74
19. Post-Retirement Postscript 2-79

Volume 3
Millennial Meditations

- MEMORIES 3-1
  - Memories of Princeton 3-3
  - Millennial Musings 3-6
- MEDITATIONS 3-9
  - Who wants to be a millionaire? 3-11
  - Shattering Shroud 3-14
  - Easter Explosion 3-16
  - Christmas Quest 3-18
- HAIKU 3-23
  - Hero Haiku 3-25
  - Haiku of Crime and Punishment 3-26
  - Apple Trees in Spring 3-29
- BIBLICAL VERSES 3-31
  - Violence Biblical and Modern 3-33
  - Two Biblical Women 3-35
  - Solomon's Reign 3-37
  - Paper Power 3-39
  - Job's Lament 3-40
  - Paul 3-42
- VISIONS 3-49
  - Serving the Other 3-51
  - Goals 3-53
  - Disciple to Apostle 3-55
  - Post-911 3-56
  - Tents 3-57

DEDICATION

Dedicated to the men of the
633rd Collection, Classification & Salvage Company,
92nd Composite Service Battalion (Keystone),
Da Nang Support Command, U. S. Army Vietnam,
1971-72

ACKNOWLEDGEMENTS

I would like to give credit to Dr. Susan Rosen for teaching my basic and advanced creative writing courses and being the faculty advisor to the student literary journal Amaranth, which published "To the tuba" in 1999 and "Mother's Schizoid Rant" in 2000. I thank Virginia Crawford for leading three poetry workshops which I attended. I thank Mary Bargteil, who led a memoir writing workshop which started me writing, is one of the leaders of the Maryland Writer's Association and coordinates all writing workshops at AACC. I want to thank the MWA journal Scribble for publishing "Our father" in 1999.

"Vietnam Junkyard" was my final paper in the Advanced Creative Writing course, which I audited in the Spring semester 2000. I appreciate the editorial comments by a fellow auditor of that course, Ted Shepherd. I had the constant support of my wife of over 30 years, Kate, our sons Ted and Michael and my daughter Julie. I thank my son Michael's friend James Bass, a Marine Reservist who served in Iraq. He read my manuscript in 2006 and his praise rekindled my enthusiasm for publishing the book.

I owe the greatest gratitude to the soldiers with whom I served in over 30 years of active and reserve service in all three categories of military personnel (enlisted, commissioned and warrant). I especially want to bring attention to support troops, which make up the majority of the forces in combat zones. Since this is a poetic work based upon my subjective memories and feelings, I have not used any names. Any opinions expressed are my own, and do not reflect the official views of the Department of Defense.

I thank Princeton Theological Seminary for publishing "Memories of Princeton" in their alumni magazine *InSpire* in May 2000 and for the publication of "Shattering Shroud" in the April 2001 edition of *Theology Today*. I thank *The Catholic Review* for printing "Disciple to Apostle" in the May 9, 2002 edition.

ABOUT THE AUTHOR

Ed Calhoon is a freelance writer, poet and retired computer specialist. He retired from the U.S. Army Reserve in 1991 as a Chief Warrant Officer with over 30 years service including 9 years on active duty and one tour in Vietnam as a Captain in the Ordnance Corps. He did graduate studies at Princeton Theological Seminary shortly after returning from Vietnam in 1972. He retired as a computer software developer for the Department of Commerce in 1997 with over 18 years of civilian service. He was advanced to his highest Reserve grade of Major, AUS Retired in 2002. He started writing poetry in 1998. His publications include an article published in *Montecito* magazine, and 14 poems published in various alumni, literary, religious and academic journals, including *Amaranth, Scribble, InSpire, Theology Today* and *Catholic Review.* He won an essay contest sponsored by the WriteItRight.com web site in 2003. His poem "Christmas Quest" was published in an interfaith international anthology on the spiritual life in 2006. He lives in Maryland with his wife Kate. He has three grown children and two grandchildren.

VOLUME 1

FIRST REFLECTIONS:

MEMORIES

Pre-Boomer Nostalgia

I. My early memories

Train trip

with my mother

and little brother

in a Pullman sleeper car.

I see black people

for the first time-

Porters on the train,

all called George

by the white passengers

after Mr. Pullman I think,

a little better than

calling them all boy.

The train takes us

"back-east"

from California

to the Midwest,

half way across the vast country

at the end of The War.

An uncle in Wisconsin

in khaki uniform

marches in a parade

in which split fingers meant victory.

Band concert

at my mother's alma mater

University of Wisconsin

impressed at the magic

of the conductor's wand

that commanded thunder crashes

from cymbals at the back of the band.

II. Pre-TV Radio

Weekday afternoons

listen to radio.

Follow the exploits

of the Lone Ranger, Sky King

and Sergeant Preston of the Yukon,

each made more stirring

by classical orchestral overtures.

Evenings listen with the family

to Fred Allen, Duffy's Tavern,

Jack Benny,

eternally 39-year-old tightwad,

and Fibber Magee and Molly

with their inevitable

closet full of noisy junk

that someone always opens.

Saturday mornings,

the Buster Brown show

with Froggy and his Magic Twanger.

Sunday mornings on the floor

with the comics spread out

as the announcer reads and comments

on the latest exploits of

Dick Tracy, Little Orphan Annie,

L'il Abner, Terry and the Pirates

and Prince Valiant among many others.

ED CALHOON

III. Going to the Movies

Rare nights in movie theater.

Giant spotlights

sweep the clouds above.

Barrage balloons

float overhead.

Free or very cheap

dishes, crockery or glassware

displayed in front of the stage.

Air conditioned theater as advertised.

On screen a larger than life

Wicked Witch in the Wizard of Oz

with bumpy green skin

that scares the wits

out of me as a little boy.

These memories are ever a part of me.

Ham Radio History

My first radio book

borrowed from my local library

in the early fifties

is a Radio Amateur's Handbook

circa the twenties

which leads me to believe

hams are still using Ford Model T

ignition coils in spark-gap Morse code transmitters.

Such rigs would cause interference

on every frequency known to man,

not to mention citations from the F.C.C.

I spend much of my junior high years

studying the Novice and Technician

license test preparation manuals, memorizing

band assignment frequencies

and schematic wiring diagrams

which I have to draw and explain

at a detailed component level.

The drawings fill my school notebook

instead of the class notes I should take.

Eventually I can draw complete

ED CALHOON

a.m. transmitters and

super-hetrodyne receivers

all vacuum tube rigs of course

since transistors are only

physicists' playthings.

War surplus radio equipment is cheap.

I ride my bike five miles

from San Gabriel to

a surplus store in Pasadena,

spend money I earn

delivering L.A. Examiner newspapers

on an old aircraft transmitter,

and companion receiver,

assorted crystals and tubes.

I also learn the hazards of high voltage

after I build power supplies to provide

the plate voltage for the tubes.

I learn to keep one hand in my pocket

and discharge filter capacitors with a screwdriver

to avoid being electrocuted by a "turned off" rig.

VIETNAM JUNKYARD AND OTHER POEMS

I take the Novice test in the summer

after finishing Junior High,

at the home of a ham

who happens to be the father

of one of my friends from school.

The F.C.C. allows

Novice tests to be administered

by General class hams at home.

I wait weeks for the license to come in the mail.

I am on cloud nine when it comes,

so happy that I jump on my bike

and ride over to busy Garvey avenue,

pull out in front of a car

force the driver to slam on her brakes.

She haa a baby in the car (pre-baby seat days),

upset with my actions and says

I could have injured the baby or myself.

My guardian angel works overtime that day.

That was exactly fifty years ago.

I have remained licensed all of that time,

although ham radio has been largely

overcome by the events of the technology revolution.

ED CALHOON

Summer of 59

(Music Academy of the West)

Mansion by the sea

in Santa Barbara

nineteen fifty nine

summer music school:

where "I take my place

as the one and only bass"

tuba, that is,

to quote the song "76 Trombones"

from *The Music Man*,

in the brass section

of the festival orchestra

and the brass chamber ensemble.

Spanish red tile roof;

formal garden walks

with young musicians

practicing outdoors

causing discordant

cacophonies in

quest of harmony,

or at least controlled

modern dissonance;

raising performances

to professional

levels of technique

and aspirations

to eventual

heights of artistry.

I study with the

trombonist and instructor

from the Juilliard School

of Music, Davis Shuman.

I also sing in the chorus

of Mozart's opera "The Magic Flute",

which was written

in the pre-tuba era.

In the weekly chamber music concerts

I even dare

to play classic solos

originally written for

other instruments

transposed to the tuba range,

due to the dearth of original

compositions for tuba.

ED CALHOON

I enjoy sitting

in the orchestra,

especially during

performances of

the great romantic

orchestral repertoire

by Berlioz, Brahms

Tchaikovsky and Wagner.

Sometimes I get so absorbed

in the beauty of the sound

that I miss my entrance

at a brass climax

due to loosing count

in the sometimes

hundreds of measures rest.

At the end of the summer,

I win the "Most Improved" award.

I can envision a musical career

in my future.

High Hopes Realized

(Mark Keppel High School Class of 1960)

It was the year of High Hopes,

the song by Sinatra

about the ant

that tried to move

the rubber tree plant,

the theme song

of our Senior Luncheon.

It was the year of

Chubby Checker

(an imitation

Fats Domino)

and his Peppermint Twist;

still a one-hit wonder

after forty years.

It was the year of destiny

for the Back-Eastern politician

with the funny-sounding

Massachusetts accent

ED CALHOON

and scandalously long hair;

the beginning of Camelot,

the reign of a handsome young king

and his French-speaking queen,

with a tragic ending

worthy of Shakespeare.

It was a time between wars,

the Cold War just simmering:

a seemingly safe time to join the Army

as a stepping stone to success,

at least for someone like me

without carfare to college,

unaware of the coming storm

in far-off Vietnam

that would eventually

suck me in and spit me out

still alive with all my limbs,

unlike so many others.

It was a time of innocence,

by today's standard perhaps,

but not without awareness

that something was going on

when girls showed up

with engagement rings

after the holiday vacation

in our sophomore year.

It was a time for guilt

(be it Protestant, Catholic or Jewish)

whether we sinned

or just thought about it.

We knew right from wrong,

though the sixties would

confuse those categories.

It was a time of high hopes

to strive and succeed,

hopes not always

or perfectly realized

as forty years passed.

We did the best we could

under the circumstances.

It is now the time to:

celebrate our survival,

our idealism somehow

still intact though tattered

ED CALHOON

after years of toil and trouble,

violence, wars and disease;

remember those passed on,

especially the names on the Wall;

and hold high hopes

for a better future

for our children, grandchildren

and generations to come.

FAMILY

Our father

Our father was:

A craftsman and

an artisan

of the Old School;

Doing a job

right the first time;

Knowing the right

from all the wrongs;

Both the notes and

words of the songs;

Rising above

the victimhood

of Depression

(Great or not so),

and of the fear

of joblessness

ED CALHOON

that went with it;

Raising his kids

long after the

normal age of

parenthood, in

foolish loving

defiance of

Economics.

Four Generations of Grandfathers, Fathers and Sons

1. Grandfathers

My grandfathers sprouted

from the Midwestern soil

covering farm lands

stretching from the eastern

to the western mountains

which under-rotated

became the Dust Bowl

and the vineyard of the

Depression Grapes of Wrath

while they respectively

plowed its furrows and healed

plowers' pain and suff'ring

with produce as payment

for the missing money.

Nineteenth century men,

they lived half through the next,

from pacifying the

west with Gatling Guns to

nuking Nagasaki.

ED CALHOON

One a loved physician;

the other a transplanted tiller

who gardened in old age

as a sunlit Californian;

sic transit Gloria

2. Father

My father was born in

the third year of the new

century, along with

the airplane, radio

and the automobile

(Ford's version anyway).

He owned a tin lizzie,

sold tires in retail stores,

sang on the radio,

cooked on a fishing boat,

painted landscapes in oils,

farmed as the dust approached,

followed the Yellow Brick

Road to the golden coast,

made parts for the bombers

used in the Second War

To End All Wars (They Said)

and lived to see Three More

(Korea, Nam and Gulf),

not to mention Moon Walks,

the baby steps into

the Brave New Age of Space.

He died unrecognized,

not recognizing us.

3. Myself

I was conceived before

the Pearl Harbor attack.

Born in the first summer

of the Second Great War.

A child of renewed hope

in a brighter future

after the clouds of war

clear away and peace reigns;

a time not yet arrived

as the century ends.

My birth coincided

with the first computers

then used to aim the guns

or drop the bombs which helped

win that War and the next,

but maybe not the one

in which I was to serve,

when we decided to

declare a victory

and withdraw (with honor).

Computers changed from swords

to plowshares which I used

in Commerce, not Defense.

4. My Brother

My brother Ron was born

on Easter Sunday of

fourty-four: new life in spring,

and a little brother

who imitated me

in almost everything

I did, although I was

A Tough Act To Follow.

We were both tuba men,

at least to start, both sang

in church choirs, and joined the

Army (in different corps)

doing electronics,

me on missiles and he

a "clerk for DOD"

(Army Security).

ED CALHOON

I'm a computer geek,

he's a chem technician.

I changed to Catholic,

he stayed Presbyterian.

I live in MaryLand,

he's a Floridian.

We joined together in

father's memorium.

5. My Sons

My two sons were born in

The Disco Seventies;

Generation Un-X

without the draft of war

to distract them from the

attainment of their goals.

Unlike each other yet

brothers nevertheless.

Teddy will always be

the oldest, tallest and

"gifted and talented"

with good looks and music.

He, like I, has been known

to over commit and

procrastinate then crash

after a midnight cram.

Michael knows exactly

what he wants and goes for

it, conscientiously

completing all of his

homework early and well,

with a computer mind

and an entrepreneur's

feel for the bottom line.

ED CALHOON

Sonnet on Mother's Dying

The end is close as sleep becomes the norm

and food is not partaken as before.

Years of paranoia and mental storm

replaced by recognizing those she bore:

we three kids who grew up as motherless

finally come to sooth our mother's brow.

Better late than never; nevertheless,

hard for others to understand "why now?",

after many years of seeming neglect.

With perfect hindsight we see, through our pain,

she could not control chemical defect

and its effect in both us and her brain.

At least we were able to end the strife

in the last stanza of the song of life.

Kate

My Katherine is

Kate not a Katie:

my mate not only

many things besides;

mother of our sons

men, but boys to her;

mistress of four cats

many rescued strays;

maternal mainly

military too;

mother to her Mum

Mum's puppy as well;

mounter of photos

mostly in albums;

mailer of missives

matted with stickers;

messy no longer

miracles ceaseless;

ED CALHOON

mountain-moving faith

many quakes involved;

Mona Lisa not

may arouse Irish;

monolithic will

must be Germanic;

my marriage partner

marvel undeserved.

ANIMALS

Two Tom Cats

(Long and short tales)

HARRISON: (Short lines for a long-hair cat)

Harrison, I call him,

or Harry or Hairy Cat

is a big black Tom Cat

full of Black Pride

(or is it just Male Ego?)

with a highly

arching back that looks

good on Halloween

next to the carved pumpkin

on the front porch.

MARS: (Long lines for a short-hair cat)

Mars is the other male cat who shares our home,

slightly cross-eyed and crazy as a loon

from growing up in a boy's bedroom,

shredding the wallpaper with his claws

and thinking he is a human who speaks in meows.

Mars is a beautiful solid blue-gray cat,

a British Blue or French Chartreux or Thai Korat

(We aren't sure because he arrived without pedigree

on a Dark and Stormy Night,

but that is Another Story).

Two Royal Felines

Puzzles The Queen:

Puzzles is pushing twenty

a centenarian in human terms

with the calico cat's patchwork coat

the command presence of a dowager queen

and a temper that is downright mean.

Her warning growl leaves no doubt

that if you mess with her

she'll scratch your eyes out.

All of the other cats in the house

obey her royal laws

and stay out of range of her claws.

ED CALHOON

Spuffy the Princess:

Spuffy is a beautiful, thin gray and white

shorthair cat whose looks have been unchanged

for over the decade or more of her life

since birth in the woodpile out back.

She is the spitting image of her Mom,

(now Dear Departed) though not as mean,

probably due to avoidance of motherhood.

Her high squeaking plaintive meowing

helps her to get her royal way.

Geoffrey the Poodle

Geoffrey is a little, 15-pound

Grey miniature poodle

Who, through no fault of his own,

Was never properly trained.

He still plays with toys like a pup,

And barks when a visitor comes

Or the phone rings.

He lived for ten years or more

With his elderly mistress,

Protecting her fiercely

And guarding his food as well

(Sometimes to the point of biting)

Until she became ill

And unable to care for him.

He misses her and she him.

They visit occaisionally,

And his puppy love bursts forth,

Unconditional and everlasting.

Theologians said animals have no soul,

But such love will not go unrewarded.

PLACES

City of Angels

I miss:

Craggy California mountains,

looming on the horizon,

visible from the beach;

Faults threatening earthquakes;

Waiting for the Big One;

Ashes from wild fires;

Mud slides when it rains;

Flash floods

racing down the arroyos to the sea,

drowning little boys

who play as did I in tunnels

leading to cement-covered river beds

(normally dry as a bone

from keeping lawns green in a desert

and quenching imagined needs

of mankind in fevered dreams

clouded by the smoke of millions

of stinking machines

taking them from

ED CALHOON

home to job and back,

maybe to a condo as well

if they are rich enough

to escape the hell

of the black or brown or yellow

homeboys' 'hoods

with barred windows

and drive-by shootings

which have progressed

from the zip guns of my day

to the Uzis of today).

Oh how I miss L.A.!

Sunset Beach

Cape May, New Jersey

Summer seashore sensations:

The feel of gritty sand between my toes;

The smell of ocean spray;

The taste of saltwater taffy;

The sight of the sun slowly setting

beyond the sunken ship's hull,

a relic of a war long past

placed there as a breakwater,

sailboat sails billowing with wind,

a ferry slowly wending it's way across the bay;

The sound of shutters clicking

as the sun touches the horizon

(in quest of the perfect photograph),

the music of the Star Spangled Banner

playing through the tinny loudspeaker on a pole

as the flag is furled, lowered and folded

by a boy scout troop

in tribute to heroes past,

ED CALHOON

who like the horseshoe crabs

whose shells are scattered on the shore

strove a season and passed on,

buried in the sand

on which we stand

and feel between our toes.

Country Church Strawberry Festival

Sun shines brightly
   in the clear blue sky
      as the band assembles
         by the country church.

Tables set out
   under the trees
      filled with fantastic food.

Barbecued chicken,
   fresh cole slaw,
      strawberry short cakes
         topped with whipped cream.

Music fills the air
   as the band begins to play;
      smells of food fill my nostrils
         and awaken my appetite
            as I toot my tuba.

Sun beams down.
      My thirst increases.
         Finally we finish.
            I drink deeply
               of cool water.

ED CALHOON

Food tastes as good

    As it looks and smells.

        I eat until full,

            Finishing with the

                Festive red berries.

Why do I live in Arnold, Maryland?

(First Prize—WriteItRight.com Essay Contest)

Arnold, Maryland in the middle

of the Mid-Atlantic

on Broadneck peninsula

created by Severn and Magothy

rivers leading to

Chesapeake Bay.

Tree-lined residential streets

bloom beautifully each spring.

Greater or lesser glimpses of the water

depending on your means.

Bounded by Ancient Annapolis

south and east,

suburban Severna Park

north and west

In the center of

Anne Arundel County

named after an English lady,

ED CALHOON

main campus of A.A.C.C.

certified by the N.A.B.

best community college

in the U. S. of A.,

where they let us kids

over the Big Six Oh

go back to school tuition free

and take workshops on

writing our memoirs, poems,

essays, plays, short stories

or Great American Novels

while trying to avoid

Snoopy's favorite opening:

"It was a dark and stormy night."

P. O. box home of

Maryland Writers Association

To which belonging

I attempt to answer

My third and final calling

After service military and civil

Allowing my beard to grow

Becoming a hirsute

Hemingway wannabe.

DISEASES

Mother's Schizoid Rant

Crazy I am not.

Imposters invaded and replaced

    each and every one of you.

My imposter husband

    is really a gigolo in disguise;

        a male prostitute.

My real oldest son ran away;

    you are too big to be my son.

My real daughter is being held hostage,

    under the next-door neighbor's porch.

My enemies become invisible,

    by covering themselves with ectoplasm.

They are plotting to steal our property

    by forcing me to sign this oil-drilling lease,

        and that mortgage loan application.

I see the Devil's Demons at night,

    but they can't hurt me

        because I am the Holy Ghost.

I hear voices telling me to take this knife

    and free my daughter.

ED CALHOON

The policemen are part of the plot;

    they are taking me back to the loony bin,

    to torture me with electric shocks,

        and tear out part of my brain

            if necessary to shut me up.

It is all very clear.

Dad's Alzheimer's

It struck Aunt Noma first:

an ex-medical technician,

floral nursery manager

expert lecturer on flower arrangement

and master bridge player.

She became unable to

manage her bank accounts

or renew her certificates of deposit.

My father became her executor,

and she spent the rest of her life

in a nursing home, dying at 94.

Then it was my father's turn:

when Noma died, he forgot

to notify some relatives,

they missed her funeral

and blamed him for the oversight.

He was stuck in the sand

in his car a mile from home,

ED CALHOON

couldn't find his way back

and was rescued after

spending the night there,

by a man who gave him

a ride on a Harley-Davidson.

He got lost driving the 200 miles

to my brother's house.

Finally he fell and broke his hip,

was found the next day

by neighbors and hospitalized.

They fixed his hip but found

his mind was unsound.

He was taken to live near

my brother, but believed

he was still near his old home.

On visits to his son's house,

he would go out the door,

thinking he could walk back.

He thought we were trying

to steal his money,

which in fact was almost gone

by the time he died.

He claimed he was Not Like Noma,

panicked that he would meet her fate.

He stopped recognizing us,

but he hung on to memories

of events 30 or more years earlier,

in his life as an artist, singer

and past master of the Reader's Digest

"It Pays to Improve Your Word Power".

He died of heart failure at 90.

Shared Surgery

Father and son skull scars,
    husband and wife abdominal zippers:
        these knit together our family
            through the tracks of healings past
                where skin was sewn to fill the gaps
                    left by cutting to remove or destroy
                        errant or overactive cells
                            caused by environmental poisons,
                                genetic inheritance
                            or the twain together.
                      Did we picket the polluters
                and/or curse our foreparents?
            Neither.
        We just thanked God
      they caught it
    and cut it
in time.

My Parkinson's

If I had to choose

a progressively disabling disease,

Parkinson's would be it;

not Lou Gherig's,

Shy-Drager's

or Jerry's Kids'.

However, it chose me

with a slight tremor

a lot of stiff muscles

and slow movements.

Treatment by L-Dopa

worked for a while,

until the side-effects

became worse than the disease.

Then came the metal

Crown of Thorns

and skull drilling

sans anesthesia,

followed by probing

and zapping the guilty

ED CALHOON

overactive brain cells,

a miraculous short-term cure

and a few years of

almost normal life;

then a gradual return

of symptoms,

now coming on the

other side of the body.

Trials of new meds,

most with no free lunch

but new side effects

to offset the gains.

Promises of a cure,

and research saying

that genes play a part,

only leading to the

fear I may have passed on

the disease to my daughter,

in addition to bipolar disease

she already got

like her cousin.

Support groups,

where many are

worse off than me,

and surgery or meds

that work for one person

don't work for another.

Claims that longevity

Is not affected by the disease,

followed by obituaries

that state the deceased

had the disease,

but died of something else

(coincidence? I think not).

Pray and pay for the cure.

ED CALHOON

Cancer Survivor

Twelve is the current number

of years, that is,

since first diagnosis

and treatment of something

gone awry in my body

who knows how or why?

It was by the grace of God

that I watched a friend

die slowly, wasting away

because of delayed diagnosis

(or maybe it was just his time to go).

Anyway, I demanded "unnecessary tests"

as a good hypochondriac,

and a technician looked

at other surrounding organs,

found an unexpected tumor

just in the nick of time.

It hadn't spread,

which was just as well,

since if it had

they wouldn't have bothered

to treat it with chemo or radiation,

just say "sayonara baby",

see you later.

I gladly went under the knife,

even volunteering to put up the date.

Five was the magic number

of hours of surgery.

Then as many months of recuperation

followed by more months

of weird twinges

and slowly healing scars.

Checkups every six months

until five years went by

without any new tumors,

and a sigh of relief.

ED CALHOON

The question still remains:

why and how did the tumor start growing?

Pollution and/or genetics?

And why did the neighbor

across the street get another kind,

as well as a friend

a mile to the west

and a daughter of friends

a mile to the east.

Could it be from living

downwind of chemical plants

fifteen miles to the north?

Or upwind of a nuclear plant

fifty miles to the south?

Or adjacent to a polluted bay?

We have more questions than answers

as we enter the new millennium.

Let us pray to become conquerors of cancer,

not merely survivors.

FUN

To The Tuba—Cinquain So Low

Tuba

The Lowest Brass

Instrument of them all

Sounds the tonic note of the chord

Solo.

ED CALHOON

A Tubist's Haiku

Forty-five years past

I arrived at Fort George Meade

to play the tuba.

Youngest member of

the Army Field Band; eighteen,

full of confidence.

I push sixty-five,

with music a link to the

passion of my youth.

Played tuba

with a community band

until my lip gave out,

probably due to Parkinson's.

Haiku on Writing

I started writing

after early retirement.

Never had more fun.

VOLUME 2

VIETNAM JUNKYARD

(AN ARMY SUPPORT-UNIT SAGA)

VIETNAM JUNKYARD AND OTHER POEMS

VIETNAM JUNKYARD

1

VIETNAM VOLUNTEER

Problems in paradise:

Army Ordnance Corps Captain

on a tropical Pacific island;

doing explosives demolition

and launch pad safety

for anti-ballistic missiles

which rendezvous with

friendly reentry vehicles

catapulted from the California coast,

while on the horizon

bob Soviet fishing trawlers

bristling with antennas, not nets

fishing for data

in the SALT[1] water

of the Cold War.

Island so small

---

[1] Strategic Arms Limitation Treaty

ED CALHOON

it is half runway,

causing claustrophobics

to take the next flight back;

like a small town

of military overseers,

civilian contractors,

and native laborers

who commute daily by boat

from the adjacent slum-island,

where they were shipped

when their home islands

were covered with mushroom clouds

and they became human fallout

of the nuclear arms race.

A perfect picture postcard:

blue lagoon,

with coral and tropical fish;

raw sewage pouring out of pipe

from that island into lagoon;

soaring suicide rate

among young native men

brought on by

missionary-converted mothers

in a matrilineal society

who will not cook for

unemployed sons

due to their beer drinking

(good subject for my paper

in night-school psych course);

Main island, at

the bottom of the atoll,

was the site

of a major battle

during World War II.

Ninety percent of the

Japanese defenders

fought to the death

rather than dishonor

their god-king Emperor.

We are called to pick up

unexploded artillery shells

found by road repair crew

in a bunker

where they also found

bones of ex-inhabitants

expired from inhalation

of napalm from flamethrowers.

Their bones were returned

to home country

almost thirty years

after their demise.

We're called by a mother-

wants us to check out

son's shell collection-

explosive shells, not seashells,

picked up on the beach.

In the kid's shoebox

we find an especially hazardous

collectible—a fully fused and intact

20-millimeter Japanese

antiaircraft artillery shell.

Struck nose first on a sidewalk,

it could have maimed or killed him.

The bottom of the lagoon

is littered with the hulks

of sunken ships

hit during the

naval bombardment

preceding the invasion.

They are popular targets

of souvenir-seeking

scuba divers

hoping to find

a ship's wheel, bell or compass.

The biggest wreck of all

Is the German battleship

that went aground

on the reef when

towed back

from h-bomb test site.

Upside-down,

full of twenty years of silt,

highly dangerous to divers.

ED CALHOON

Two of my fellow captains

scuba dive on the battleship,

neglect to use a safety line.

Their fins kick up the silt,

causing disorientation.

They run out of air

and drown.

The junk of war

claims victims 30 years later.

My troubled marriage,

held together for my child's sake,

because I want to watch

my golden-haired girl grow up,

slowly steams in the tropical

small-town social pressure cooker.

We keep the lid on as proper Presbyterians,

which leads to a Christmas trip

to Baltimore and a second separation—

beginning of the end.

I stay in bachelor quarters for a few months,

play trombone in a band,

direct a musical for fun,

take a scuba diving course;

come down with mono

after I swallow lagoon water,

not by a kiss for sure.

I volunteer for Vietnam

in waning days of the war

("Only war we've got",

said a Major mentor).

I say I do it for

combat pay

tax breaks

and colored ribbons

that might lead to promotion.

I may have a little touch

of semi-suicidal depression

at the prospect of failing

the critical life task of marriage.

Can it be a coincidence

that when we first separated,

I volunteered for hazardous

Explosive Disposal duty,

and now I volunteer for Vietnam?

2
Flight to Nam

I take leave en route in the Midwest

where as a child I lived

for a year under the watchful eyes

of Aunt Noma and Uncle Sam

(his real name, not the guy in the poster),

stern farmers both,

real-life *American Gothics*

without kids of their own,

substitute parents for us three,

little brother, littler sister and me

(all of eight, six and three)

when our mother was

non compos mentis,

in an asylum by another name

(sanitarium) a shocking institution,

in more ways than one,

our family secret well concealed

to cover the shame within.

VIETNAM JUNKYARD AND OTHER POEMS

There I meet

a soldier just back

from Nam, recuperating

after being shot down

in his helicopter

(I never trusted flying

in something that glides

like a rock and is low and slow

enough to be sometimes

brought down by ground fire;

so much for "air superiority.")

I fly in my first 747

from Minneapolis to Seattle,

remember past trips there:

in sixty-two to play the tuba

with the touring Army Field Band

at the World's Fair,

in sixty-three to fly to Fairbanks

to start my tour as a missile technician;

in sixty-four drive through

with my new bride

ED CALHOON

after slip-sliding

all the way down

the Al-Can Highway

in November like a dumb-ass,

on my way to

Aberdeen, Maryland

to attend the Ordnance School's

technologically elite

Calibration course.

I push thirty

as a junior captain with

too much time

and not enough

ribbons on my chest.

With the draft-dodging

rampant in the reserves and guard,

it doesn't help

if I explain how I spent

the peak combat years

as a Calibration Instructor

and in the reserves

while attending college

on the Vietnam version

of the GI Bill.

We fly Great Circle:

first to Anchorage,

which I last saw in sixty-four,

right after the big earthquake

when they bulldozed

most of downtown

and I helped fix up missile sites;

then Japan,

the vanquished former enemy

now rebuilt and booming;

the Philippines,

former prize of war

lost and retaken by McArthur

upon his promised return,

whose "old soldiers never die"

speech I heard

over Aunt Noma's radio

twenty years earlier;

finally Cam Ranh Bay,

largest port facility in the Pacific.

In country at last, hoping not to be

the last to die before the lights go out.

3
CAM RANH BAY

The first thing I feel

is the humidity;

constant and oppressive,

unlike the island

with its nearly constant trade winds.

I sweat through my khakis

in less than an hour.

We are issued jungle fatigues and boots

at a supply tent on the beach.

We put away our khakis,

shiny brass, shoes and belt buckles

all of which could make us

better targets for snipers;

sew on black insignia

and get black on green name tapes,

all the better to blend in the jungle.

Pack away the khakis for

Rest and Relaxation (R&R) leave,

in six months (halfway through the tour).

We are segregated in the Replacement Center,

as "newbies" or "long-timers";

"Short timers" are those with

less than 100 days left in country

("double digit midgets"),

and everybody has a calendar

marked with days left;

the main goal is survival.

I check in with the officer assignment clerk,

am disappointed to hear that the

EOD Detachment (bomb squad)

that I was to command

has been deactivated as the pullout proceeds,

and I am forced to forage for an assignment.

I am also given the latest news:

An EOD top sergeant died

in a jeep accident;

those damn M-151 jeeps,

with their automobile-like independent suspensions,

tip over suddenly on curves

without any seat-of-the-pants feel,

unlike the old M-38 models

(newer isn't always better);

another example of

latest technology,

like the M-16 rifles

that don't work in mud and sand

as well as the cruder

Communist AK-47s.

I see Vietnamese civilians for the first time,

entertainers in the makeshift Officers Club,

trying to sound like an American band.

During the daytime, I see

mostly women who work as maids

in the "hooches"

(shacks constructed from boxes,

and other scrap lumber),

providing cheap laundry,

shoe shines and "other duties as assigned"

(the military catchall category,

that covers a multitude of sins, literally).

I am a lonely stranger in a foreign land,

not knowing local language or lore.

VIETNAM JUNKYARD AND OTHER POEMS

A clerk gives me orders to report

to Da Nang Support Command

on the coast up north,

for further reassignment.

I go to the airfield for a flight,

first to Saigon,

then change planes

to a cargo plane headed

up to DaNang, along with

a bunch of Vietnamese civilians

carrying their cargo in their hands

and wearing conical straw coolie hats.

I don't know their language.

I'm not sure if or how I can help them.

Anyway, it is their country, not mine.

All I can do is do my best

and hope for the best.

They address me as "dai hui", Captain.

I land in Da Nang,

to start my tour.

4
KEYSTONE BATTALION

I report to the Support Command

Personnel officer,

who tells me there is no EOD slot vacant,

but there is a Maintenance Officer job

in the Keystone Battalion,

a maintenance general support unit

reassigned to process the equipment

of the units leaving country

as part of the pullout.

The battalion commander,

a black lieutenant colonel

who looks like an ex-football player.

briefs me on the unit mission;

says he needs me now as a staff officer,

but will need some new company commanders soon.

Company commanders

spend six months

in command;

barely enough to learn the job,

punch your ticket

and receive the right ribbons

for promotion.

Soldiers know:

commanders come and go;

loyalty is a

two-way street;

and commanders' careers

mean less than soldiers' lives.

Hence the recent spate of fraggings

(fragmenation grenades

used by our boys

against their fearless leaders)

which I hope to avoid,

being in a rear-area support unit.

The colonel asks if I am interested

in a company command,

and I, an ambitious reserve officer

bucking for a regular commission,

eagerly volunteer.

The colonel introduces me

to the Executive Officer,

a major with a thin mustache,

and a stickler for detail;

ED CALHOON

the bad cop to the colonel's good cop.

The major runs the Battalion Headquarters,

while the colonel roams the area in his jeep,

putting out fires in the companies.

I move into an officer hooch

and meet the three company commanders,

living apart from their companies;

I question (to myself) the appropriateness

of commanders not living with their troops.

Over the summer, I see

the Three Musketeers (their own name)

have daily afternoon dalliances

with Vietnamese hooch maids;

it is common knowledge,

and may be seen as

officer special privileges

by the troops who work

sixteen-hour days in the wilting heat.

On Sundays, the major conducts

Officer Call over breakfast

at the China Beach R&R Center O Club,

on the white coral sand beach,

looking east at the South China Sea

and north at Da Nang Bay,

with green tree-covered

Monkey Mountain looming above.

This could be a wonderful resort, I think.

I often drive the main road

from the battalion to the port docks,

past a Vietnamese Amputees' Hospital.

On bad days, patients give

passing American vehicles

curses and, it is rumored,

throw frags.

In front of the Da Nang Depot compound

is a disheveled young woman,

with uncombed hair

and torn dress

talking to herself,

deserted by her senses and

by an American boyfriend

who left country.

ED CALHOON

I hear about an orphanage
where "Amer-Asian" children are kept,
fathered by long-gone soldiers
and unwanted by the Vietnamese.
I cannot bring myself to visit them.

As we American GIs drive through
the villages on the road to the port,
bands of street boys lurk,
waiting for the opportunity
to snatch anything not tied down.
We are told not to shoot them,
for fear of causing an international incident,
as one Master Sergeant did
when he shot a boy for stealing his watch.

The JAG lawyers accept claims
for stolen property, as well as acting as
bag men to pay for damages to civilians.
Said friendly local civilians
are in the habit of forming protest groups
after especially egregious incidents,
taking hostages and holding them
until properly compensated.

They also get unruly during elections.
All Americans are restricted
to our bases for the duration
of the political campaign.

We don't know why we aren't loved
for preventing this domino from falling to Communism.
We are treated more like German occupiers
than American liberators
in the last Good War.

As the hot summer wears on
I learn about the battalion,
consisting of three companies:
Light Equipment, Heavy Equipment
and Collection, Classification and Salvage.
The Heavy Equipment company
is commanded by an Ordnance Officer Basic
classmate of mine, recently arrived.
My choice of unit to command:
The Light Equipment company,
where I could use my electronics background.
The colonel's choice:
the Collection, Classification and Salvage company;

ED CALHOON

(the Cannibalization Point-

military jargon for junk yard),

manned by problem people—

mostly draftee combat troops

with time left on their tour

reassigned from departing units,

the human junk of the stand-down.

He says my prior enlisted service

makes me the best man for the job.

I hope to convince him otherwise.

My entire career has been spent

with elite, educated Regular Army

(not to mention clean)

volunteer units, the exact opposite

of the Salvage company.

5
DA NANG JUNKYARD

As the summer nears an end,
The colonel selects me to command
Salvage Company,
junk yard for northern
South Vietnam (their I Corps).
Housed in permanent buildings
on Tien Sha Vietnamese Navy Base,
half-way out the peninsula around the bay
between China Beach and the port docks.

About a month before taking over,
I move to the Tien Sha BOQ
to be closer to the company.
The buildings date
to French colonial days,
with stucco walls, high ceilings
and ceiling fans to provide relief
from the tropical heat by ventilation.

ED CALHOON

I meet the company supply sergeant,

always a good person to know,

for if he is any good he will be a scrounger,

procuring the normally unattainable

in spite of the Army supply system.

He like most noncoms

in the company drinks a lot;

what else to do at night?

The center of the junkyard is the Mud Pit,

holding area for damaged vehicles—

jeeps, trucks, tanks

and Armored Personnel Carriers (APCs)

shot up or wrecked in and around combat.

Those with good frames are stripped

of usable parts and unnecessary metal,

washed with high-pressure water blasters,

loaded on flatbed trailers and carried

out to the port docks for loading on

returning commercial cargo ships,

and shipment to rebuild depots.

Usable parts are rebuilt by a

Korean contract company.

VIETNAM JUNKYARD AND OTHER POEMS

Scrap metal and unrepairable frames

are sold locally; little is wasted.

The local civilians construct

whole villages from our castoffs.

As the last unit leaves

each American compound,

the local civilians dismantle

and carry off everything they can,

like ants carrying twigs and leaves back to the nest.

The outgoing company commander

is a twenty-one year old Captain,

the product of OCS right out of high school

and accelerated promotions,

only possible in the inflated wartime Army

about to be deflated by a needle

called RIF (Reduction In Force),

the selection boards for which

are just now convening.

I remember back to the pre-Vietnam Army,

when it took at least 5 years to make Captain.

I also remember serving with WWII and Korean vets,

many ex-officers serving as sergeants

just to earn their pension after earlier RIFs;

these kids don't appreciate what they got.

ED CALHOON

The young captain idolizes General Patton,

And imitates him

down to his pearl-handled revolver

and swagger stick

(the height of officer class arrogance,

in my ex-enlisted mind).

I sit beside him in the O Club

watching the movie of the same name,

as he mouths Patton's words

about the glory of war

(he can have my share of the glory).

He invites me to mount his gun truck,

a cannibalized dump truck

with an aluminum APC body hoisted on the bed

and a .50-caliber machine gun mount,

which he uses to provide fire support

while towing in the Hai Van Pass.

I pass on his offer, with the wisdom

of more years of experience,

leading to self-preservation,

not wanting to shoot and be shot at

in an unauthorized combat action.

The gun truck is just one of many
retrograde vehicles:
cannibalized trucks and jeeps,
put together with parts of two or more
junked vehicles written off the supply system
as combat losses, thus on no one's property books.

American ingenuity sees a need and fills it,
now that the supply system has ground to a halt,
as the withdrawal nears its end.

The day before the change of command ceremony,
the young captain takes his jeep,
driving himself (against command policy),
hits and injures a Vietnamese civilian,
and is promptly surrounded by a mob,
held hostage until bailed out by the bag man,
a JAG lawyer acting like
an insurance claims agent.
The jeep is set ablaze in the process,
another candidate for cannibalization.

ED CALHOON

Change of command day finally comes,

with the formal passing of the unit flag

from old to new commander.

A unit party follows,

revealing much about the unit.

The ex-college students:

draftees often with degrees

who could have been officers

had they the inclination

to volunteer for ROTC or OCS;

big men on campus

around the time of Kent State;

now drinking sodas

and eating munchies,

as pot-heads were alleged to do,

listening to psychedelic rock and roll.

The ROTC lieutenants,

their college contemporaries,

socialize and probably fraternize

with those troops

(against regulations).

The black troops are apart,

many with modified afros,

trimmed to borderline Army length,

towels around their necks

exchanging black power

handshakes and salutes,

listening to rhythm and blues.

.

The blue-collar white kids

Form the next faction,

drinking beer,

listening to country music.

A few of the men wear their fatigues

with sleeves rolled down

in spite of the heat,

covering tell-tale

needle tracks from heroin use:

labled as the "smack freaks";

first suspects in cases of petty thefts,

subject to rough barracks justice.

The sergeants are together:

many drinking heavily,

bitter about changes in the Army

from the old brown shoe days

when an NCO could rule his men

with his foul mouth and fists;

the smartest aware

that the old days are gone forever;

most afraid of the strange young troops.

The warrant officers sit apart,

respected technicians risen through the ranks;

ex-sergeants usually without college

with a foot in both the enlisted

and officer camps.

During the party

I sense a lot of tension:

draftees calling sergeants "lifers";

black power advocates

opposing the oppression of The Man;

ex-student radicals

spouting Marxist critiques

of the Military-Industrial Complex,

calling all sergeants and officers pigs

and muttering veiled threats

about what will happen

Come The Revolution.

To add fuel to this fire,

the colonel tells me

Support Command Headquarters

is demanding improvement

of military uniforms and haircuts.

As the war winds down,

we are returning to peacetime

garrison-duty life

with weekly haircuts,

spit-shined boots

and neatly pressed uniforms

(just like the pre-Vietnam Army

I first joined back in 1960).

Just what many of my men

don't want to hear,

after spending half of their tour

in a combat unit in the bush,

often stripped to the waist

covered with mud

no haircuts for months

and allowed to grow

the sideburns and mustaches

that are in style back home.

ED CALHOON

The first sergeant,

my top enlisted man,

ex-heavyweight boxer

(broken nose),

tall as me and fifty ponds heavier.

I let him run the company admin.

and be the bad cop;

I'll sign papers and

manage the mission.

In return, I'll make him

walk on water in his efficiency reports

and recommend him for promotion.

The colonel says

company command

should be the best time of my career,

with the greatest chance

of accomplishing a mission

with direct control over men and materiel.

I plunge in with mixed feelings

of enthusiasm and apprehension;

aware of my shortcomings

as a leader of men

in contrast to my technical background,

but hoping to look out

for the welfare of my men

and somehow be rewarded

for doing my best

in a thankless situation.

ED CALHOON

6
Wash Rack Crew

The most thankless task

in the salvage company

is working on the wash rack.

The old wrecked vehicles

are pulled over to the water blasters

and washed down

with high-pressure water.

Ammunition and grenades

are placed in the EOD pickup box.

Human remains (body parts)

are given to graves registration.

The water is pumped from the bay,

the mouth of a long river

into which countless villages

empty their raw sewage.

As a result, the men

suffer from skin diseases,

possible Agent Orange runoffs

and innumerable unnamed maladies

caused by the contents

of the water which soaks their bodies.

VIETNAM JUNKYARD AND OTHER POEMS

Next to the washrack

is the holding yard

for the junk vehicles,

dubbed the Mud Pit.

I stand ankle-deep in mud

when a CS (tear gas) grenade

pops upwind,

followed by a white cloud

that descends upon the pit

and me without

my Protective Mask.

I proceed to catch a full dose,

clear my sinuses

and loose my lunch.

It was probably a prank

pulled by the wash rack crew,

using a grenade from the EOD box.

Or was it part of the pattern

of equipment sabotage

and marijuana smoking

motivated either by malingering

or political subversion

by ex-student radicals?

ED CALHOON

I read about a general

given a Silver Star

for flying over a battle

in a Huey (helicopter).

The brass react

to congressional criticism

by pressuring commanders

to nominate deserving enlisted men

for awards and decorations,

perhaps going overboard

in the opposite direction.

I nominate the wash rack crew,

and one day we stand in formation

in front of the wash rack

as a general alights from his Huey

to pin 45 Army Commendation Medals

on the cleaned-up chests of the crew.

The irony for me

is that when I was enlisted

the officers got most of the medals.

Until recently combat zone commanders

got Bronze Stars (less V);

now the tables are turned,

and I have only my

Good Conduct ribbon,

red with white stripes,

and two metal knots

that says I did 2 enlistments (6 years)

without getting caught screwing up.

7
INSPECTIONS (HAIRCUTS, UNIFORMS AND DRUGS)

Next to shipping out salvage,

the most important mission

given me as a commander

is inspecting the troops

for proper "uniforms and appearance".

I am aided in this mission

by the Military Police

who issue tickets called DRs,

for which I am supposed to give

non-judicial punishment (Article 15).

I am given a quota

of a court-martial for every 3 DRs,

disregarding whether there is

sufficient evidence for conviction.

For recurring drug cases,

I am to request

administrative discharges

and let the Veterans Administration

treat them back in the real world.

VIETNAM JUNKYARD AND OTHER POEMS

Some soldiers extend their tours

to keep the cheap drug supply,

readily available in the villages.

I walk over from the BOQ

in the evening

and smell the marijuana smoke

being forced out of the barracks

with cross-ventilating standing fans.

I can confiscate any drugs I find,

but can't prosecute

unless I have probable cause for search,

just like a cop in civilian life.

I can only have probable cause

if a snitch tells me exactly where to look,

like a good police informant,

which would probably be

the first and last time

I could use the informant.

The troops arrange their bunks

with hanging blankets and beads

forming passageways

f or marijuana smoke.

ED CALHOON

Marijuana is less of a problem

than heroin and alcohol,

since it usually doesn't lead

to crime and violence.

However, I crack down

on everything illegal,

expecting some reaction

but not knowing its nature.

In a daily inspection in the ranks,

I order a soldier to get a haircut.

He does not comply in a few days,

and appeals to the Battalion Commander

to overturn my order.

The colonel also tells him to get a haircut,

and he complies but I can tell

that he is really riled

at being challenged to change

after spending so much time in the bush

doing as he wished with his hair.

A short cocky kid,

an ex-helicopter door gunner,

dislikes wearing his uniform top,

preferring instead to strip to the waist.

He wants to get out of the Army,

by any means possible.

He enters the base theater

to watch a movie.

The group commander

and deputy, both bird colonels,

spot him and order him

to go back to the barracks

and put on his uniform top.

He walks out of the theater,

and reenters by another door

still out of uniform.

The colonels see him again,

and have MPs arrest him

for disobeying a direct order

(a court-martial offense).

The two colonels are short-timers,

so they give the JAG a deposition.

The colonels return to the states,

and the young soldier

gets a smart young JAG lawyer

ED CALHOON

who challenges the deposition

because there was no cross-examination.

The poor kid can't even get kicked out

of the Army to save his life.

8
FRAGGINGS

Just before morning formation

one of the sergeants notices

a coffee can on the ground

next to the wall

of the company headquarters building,

just behind where I stand each morning.

He looks in the can

and sees a fragmentation grenade

wrapped with electrical tape

with the pin pulled

submerged in gasoline

(an old VC trick)

making a crude but effective

chemical time delay bomb

which will explode

when the tape disintegrates.

The sergeant brings me the grenade.

I tell him to hold on to the grenade

tightly to keep the handle from flying off

and put a pin or nail in the hole

to disarm the device.

I am shaken as I think about the close call.

The scene is repeated twice,

once at the First Sergeant's room

and again at another sergeant's room.

One of the two other company commanders

also has a fragging that almost succeeds:

his hootch wall is blown down

but the wall absorbed the fragments.

As a result of the fragging attempts,

the colonel offers to transfer my

five most likely suspects.

I dislike passing problems on

to another unit as a general rule,

but I give him the names of five

suspected smack freaks,

who are swiftly transferred.

The Military Police investigate,

but are initially unable to

identify the culprit(s).

I figure I angered someone

with my drug busts.

9
PLAIN CLOTHES POLICE

There are two kinds

of plain clothes military

investigators skulking around

pretending to be civilians

while wearing pistol belts

and six-guns like cowboys,

sticking out from the crowd

instead of blending in

(real civilian contractors

don't wear pistol belts.)

One type is Criminal Investigation Division (CID),

part of the Military Police;

the other is Counter Intelligence Corps (CIC),

part of Army Intelligence

(an oxymoron to many).

The CID agents earn their pay

hanging around bars

listening for incriminating intimations.

They hear the man with haircut issues

brag about trying to blow me away.

ED CALHOON

I was shocked and stunned to learn

that I was almost killed

over the length of sideburns,

not for busting drugs as I had supposed.

I don't understand why hair length

is so important

for my Baby Boomer troops.

I kept my hair short,

and wore a flat-top

all through high school

and by habit through

the decade of the sixties,

only allowing my sideburns

to creep down to the

Army limits and my hair

to grow long enough to comb

as the seventies started.

The CIC agents show up

to investigate the loyalty

of a young private

just out of basic training

and recently arrived in country

whose crime is having

a Slavic name

and relatives behind the Iron Curtain.

After questioning his

sergeant and fellow soldiers,

the investigators insure

that he is covered

with a cloud of suspicion

as they return repeatedly

with no evidence of wrongdoing.

ED CALHOON

10
Problems with alcohol

A sergeant staggers

into the orderly room

waves a broken bottle

and babbles about

his wife's request

for a divorce

in a recently received

Dear John letter.

I retreat to my office,

tell the First Sergeant

to try to handle the situation

without bringing charges

if at all possible.

Alcohol and emotions are an explosive mix.

Nothing comes of the incident.

After leaving the enlisted club

across the main highway from the Navy base

thoroughly soused, three of my men

enter the base through the guard gate.

They get in a fight with the Navy guard,

grab his gun and it goes off,

wounding the guard in the process.

The men run away in panic,

and hide in the nearby village.

I conduct an investigation

and notify the MPs about the incident.

Relations with the Navy units

on the base are strained

to say the least.

We were unpopular to start,

what with towing and trucking

loads of old junk vehicles

up the road to the docks,

but this makes us

persona non grata.

I fear that the men involved

might stay in the village

after the unit disbands,

leaving them men without a country.

Eventually they return

to face the charges and costs

ED CALHOON

of a night of intoxication.

On another night

a sergeant drinks himself

into a stupor.

He passes out.

I am told

that he is sick.

I put him on a stretcher

and take him by jeep to

China Beach Evacuation Hospital.

The medics say

he is just drunk.

All things considered,

I have more problems

with alcohol than pot.

Pot smokers tend

to be passive.

Many of the sergeants

are alcoholics

but the Army social culture

uses booze to celebrate

promotions, transfers, retirements,

Dining In ceremonies for regimental rapport.

11
EVACUATION HOSPITAL

A welder uses his

torch to cut up

a junk truck.

The fuel tank

is empty

but the torch

ignites residual fumes

causing an explosion

injuring the welder.

The initial report

I receive

is a possible

VC grenade attack-

man wounded

transported to

China Beach

Evacuation Hospital.

I visit him there.

Learn he will be

evacuated to Japan.

ED CALHOON

Personally pick up

his personnel, finance

and medical records.

Find out that

he has not been paid

for several months,

due to lost records.

Ask First Sergeant

to find out if any

other troops

have pay problems.

During visits to

the Evac hospital,

notice easy-going

relations between

enlisted medics and officer nurses.

I stare at the nurses,

first American women

I've seen in country.

Easy to see how

soldier patients

could be entranced.

12
Chapel

I'm only officer

from my battalion

attending chapel.

Try to avoid

appearance of

favoritism towards

men that attend chapel.

One of the men

in the bible study group

is a Navy junior petty officer

who calls himself

a Charismatic Catholic,

a category of which I was unaware.

He speaks like a Protestant Pentecostal,

praising God in all circumstances,

a ray of light

in an otherwise dismal situation.

It seems to me that

Vatican II has started

A real renewal in the old church.

ED CALHOON

I meet our

Battalion Chaplain.

He is the only

Eastern Orthodox priest

in all of U.S. Army Vietnam.

He does not have enough

Orthodox troops to

justify a separate chapel,

So he just travels around

the country visiting

individual Orthodox soldiers.

He seems lonely.

We talk about

chaplaincy and

his seminary experience.

Told him I had thought

about seminary,

Even visited Princeton Seminary

back in the early sixties

when I was on tour

with the Army Field Band.

Only one

American woman

comes to chapel,

a Red Cross worker

(nicknamed "Donut Dollies"

by earlier generations

of soldiers).

After services

she attracted a large

group of soldiers.

I hesitate to

talk to her

for fear of seeming

to pull rank,

or just be another

sex-starved soldier,

like those frequenting

the massage parlors

near the gates

of most bases.

Unit commanders

and chaplains

are directed to discourage

marriages between

American troops

and local civilians.

ED CALHOON

13
Feeling Unappreciated

As I drive my own jeep

to the China Beach PX

(against command policy,

same as my predecessor),

I stop at the intersection

behind a jeep full of

Vietnamese Rangers.

One of them jumps off,

walks back to my jeep

and spits in my face,

then returns to his jeep

with a grin on his face.

I am outnumbered and outgunned,

so I can do nothing but take it.

Again I feel like a German officer

in occupied France during WWII,

despised by the inhabitants.

I return to the states on R&R leave,

flying to Saigon first,

stopping there for a short time,

taking a rickshaw

and leaving my briefcase

in the conveyance

with my airline tickets.

I am frantic,

and finally contact the

rickshaw driver

and pay a ransom

for my belongings.

I fly to Honolulu and then

back to Baltimore

and visit my dear daughter.

During my leave,

I also visit my career counselor

at Officer Personnel Operations

in the Tempo (WWII temporary) buildings

at Fort McNair in DC.

My counselor tells me

I am selected

for the Reduction in Force (RIF),

to be mustered out in a few months.

No college degree

was probably a factor,

even though I am only

one semester away.

Also there is only one Major slot

for every ten Captain slots in EOD.

They want people to volunteer

For hazardous duty,

but don't provide

potential for advancement.

The fact that I am in

my first combat zone assignment

and first command

and have not yet been

given an efficiency report

is irrelevant-

I have too many strikes against me.

I return to Nam after the leave,

notify the new colonel,

the old one having been replaced

at the end of his command tour.

I volunteer to cut my command tour short,

and allow someone else

to get his ticket punched;

my active duty career is almost over

and I will return to the reserves.

The change of command

does not include any awards.

My command efficiency report

by the colonel says

that I succeeded in difficult circumstances

where others had failed.

However, the group commander's

endorsement says that I don't provide enough

Open Door office time for the men.

This is the first time

I hear such a criticism.

All of the command pressure

was on the mission:

cutting the Mud Pit backlog

and shipping the maximum metal.

Such a comment from an endorser

is the kiss of death

for a career, as is anything

less than perfection.

ED CALHOON

14
Ammo Officer

My RIF order

is lost in the chain of command.

Support Command Personnel reassigns me

to the Ammunition Officer slot

for the Fifth Transportation Command,

which runs the Da Nang Port.

I am in charge of the temporary Ammunition

storage yard for the port at the Bridge Ramp.

My workers are Vietnamese civilians,

supervised by Korean contractors,

making for a multilingual/cultural mélange.

The contractors are my clerks,

and add atmosphere

from the fragrance of

pickled kimchi (fermented cabbage)

laden with garlic

which hits me in the nostrils

as soon as I enter the office.

The Koreans are all college grads,

and very industrious.

They invite me to eat lunch

VIETNAM JUNKYARD AND OTHER POEMS

with them at a Korean restaurant.

I even try Kimchi

and develop a taste for it,

but the garlic odor

emanates from my body for days.

A Vietnamese woman checker

introduces me to her brother,

a Vietnamese Army Major.

They invite me and another Captain

to their family Tet

holiday celebration.

There we meet the family patriarch,

their father, a veteran

of the wars with the Japanese

and French, who had been

evacuated to the south after

the partition of the country.

The family is Catholic,

typical of the southern leadership.

The history of the country

is visible in this family.

Korean boat crews carry ammo

in landing craft

from the commercial cargo ships

ED CALHOON

at anchor in the bay

to my temporary storage area

at the landing ramp.

Vietnamese stevedores store it

in open bays with sand bag walls.

The fork lifts and milvans (military trailers)

are in poor shape,

and the stevedores are sloppy.

One uses a fork lift

to hold up the end of a milvan

with a broken landing leg

while loading the van

with propane tanks.

The van falls,

spilling the load

starting a fire in the ammo

and burning a guard tower.

We think we are under attack,

and radio the headquarters

which sends helicopters to reconnaissance.

After the incident,

scuba gear is found

hidden under the dock,

making a real enemy attack

a possibility.

There are also nighttime

rocket attacks,

launched from the perimeter

and not very accurate,

but reminding me

that I am in a combat zone

as I wear my flack jacket

in the bomb shelter.

I start the paperwork

to complete my college degree

in summer school

and enter Princeton Seminary

in the fall.

I arrange to take the

required tests

at the Army Education Center.

ED CALHOON

The night before my departure

From DaNang, I meet a classmate

from my EOD course,

a Captain assigned to MACV

(Military Assistance Command).

I go to the MACV O Club with him

for a farewell dinner with a friend.

We tell stories about our time in country.

On his pistol belt

is hanging

a miniature hand grenade

the size of a golf ball

which he got from

Special Operations unit

performing "dirty tricks"

on or maybe over

the DMZ border

between North and

South Vietnam.

VIETNAM JUNKYARD AND OTHER POEMS

I get really drunk

for the first time in my life,

(at age 29 going on 30).

When I return to the BOQ,

the room seems to take

a 180 degree turn

and I lose my dinner.

ED CALHOON

15
RETURN TO THE WORLD

I fly back the way I came,

contract flight over the pole via

the Philippines,

Japan and Alaska

to Seattle.

Then by commercial plane to

California to visit relatives.

In L.A., I see a news report

about a big attack in Da Nang.

Out in the nick of time, I think.

I return to Maryland for a final

assignment prior to discharge

at good old Fort Meade.

I enroll in the coming summer school

to finish my college degree,

and am conditionally accepted

for seminary admission in the fall.

Then came Change Number Two,

all discharges are frozen

for six months:

SNAFU for sure.

I apply for and get an exception.

I get no parades or medals,

just a piece of paper

and some cardboard certificates

suitable for framing,

telling me of the gratitude

of my country.

ED CALHOON

16

BE ALL YOU CAN BE
IN THE ARMY RESERVE

I return to the reserves,

using weekend drills and

annual summer camps

as a part-time job

to supplement the meager

G. I. Bill benefits

while finishing my college

and going on to graduate schools

in counseling and divinity,

considering a career

in pastoral counseling

or chaplaincy (military or hospital).

I get a chance to go

to the Ivy League,

as a Presbyterian at Princeton

(Seminary, that is,

next door to the U. Grad. School),

be bedazzled by the fancy footwork

of serious world-class scholars

and adopt an ambivalent attitude

about neo-orthodox theology

and biblical languages,

which masks my calling confusion.

After dropping out twice,

remarriage (to a Catholic

WAC reserve lieutenant),

the birth of my boy

and a church internship,

not to mention being treated

as an almost-chaplain

by my fellow reservists,

I discover that

the clergy is not my calling.

In the process, I return to Maryland,

discover data processing as my forte

and prepare to be a programmer.

I make Major,

while my wife and I serve

in the same unit.

I outrank her but she has

Command Voice

(Have no doubt

who is in charge.)

ED CALHOON

17
CALL ME MISTER ED

After the birth of our second son, my wife drops out

of the reserve unit.

Once I complete 20 years,

I do the same

and take a mobilization designee

slot in the Pentagon

for summer training only.

Majors are mere action officer trainees,

while Colonels are in charge of a

half-dozen people in a tiny office,

compared to the thousands

they command in the field.

I write and coordinate a complete staff paper

on the future use of Personal Computers

and find out later that it was changed

by a young fast-burner Lieutenant Colonel.

I don't need this

I say to myself,

and put together the paperwork

for appointment as a Chief Warrant Officer,

a reduction in rank but an increase in respect.

Warrant officers are

betwixt and between

enlisted and officer status,

wearing enameled bars

similar to a lieutenant's,

usually ex-sergeants

with a single specialty

and enormous expertise,

unable to command

(except detachments or bands),

addressed as "Mister"

or informally "Chief",

in the Army anyway

(the Navy and Marines

differ as usual.)

I saw Warrants in action

as band directors,

guided missile technicians,

calibration team leaders,

ammunition supply platoon leaders

and maintenance shop supervisor.

I will be a data processing technician,

based on my civilian experience.

ED CALHOON

Some think me crazy

to take a demotion,

giving up the constant quest

for upward mobility.

I see over-age in grade

fast approaching

as a major, but no age limit

for warrants.

I receive the appointment,

and buy new brass.

The next summer,

I report to Fort Meade

for mobilization training;

an active duty sergeant

who knew me previously

comments that I have

suddenly become smarter.

Summers come and go,

each year putting on my uniform

and reporting first to Fort Meade,

then Fort Lee, the Naval Academy

(a green suit among the blue)

and finally back to Fort Meade,

changing mobilization slots

with each reorganization

the military is wont to do.

As communism falls

and the peace dividend looms,

cuts are made eliminating

my mobilization slot with others,

and I start feeling pains

shoot through my knees

after doing my Physical Training

exercises (calisthenics),

and I have trouble doing

the annual required PT test.

My physical exam

diagnosis is arthritis,

the old man's disease,

and the military is

a place for the young and athletic,

not the old and arthritic,

although my job is mostly

wrestling with program problems,

not evil enemies.

The paper work for my retirement

is started just after the Panama operation

involving a reserve callup.

18
Fading Away

To paraphrase General McArthur,
old soldiers never retire,
they just fade away.
As tensions mount in the Gulf,
all retirements are put on hold,
as reservists are alerted
for call-ups as members of units
or individuals like me.

My cousin in Wisconsin
is called with his unit,
and my wife's cousin in Montana
is called as an individual.
As the buildup continues
I volunteer to help out,
and they turn me down
because of my disability
but still won't retire me.
During the buildup,
I join in prayers in church
for the safety of the troops.
A new spirit of support

on the home front

rises, reminiscent of WWII.

Generals Schwartzkopf and Powell

focus on the lessons learned

from their experiences in Vietnam:

that our national interests must be at stake

and adequate resources must be committed

before war is begun.

Finally, in the first week

of actual shooting

they send me my retirement order.

I fill out a form

requesting a retirement ceremony.

I watch the unfolding war

with fascination,

noticing the differences with Vietnam:

differences in uniforms, equipment and tactics

related to a desert campaign,

more like the North Africa campaigns

of the last Big War

than Nam's jungle bush battles,

rice paddy skirmishes and river operations.

The conclusion of the Gulf War,

with a minimum of casualties,

ED CALHOON

the liberation of Kuwait

and the use of a multinational coalition

promises a legacy of lessons learned

that will replace the bitter aftertaste

of loosing the Vietnam War,.

and ratify the wisdom

of the all-volunteer military.

I am moved to tears by

the welcoming home ceremonies

and parades at the end of the war,

which contrast with

the conspicuous absence

of recognition after Vietnam.

A couple of months later,

the reserve personnel center

sends me another packet

with the same old cardboard

Certificates Suitable for Framing

that I had received on discharge from active duty,

with no award for good performance

and no mention of a retirement ceremony.

An old colonel told me once

that you have to be your own

personnel manager

in an impersonal Army.

So I send a letter re-requesting

a retirement ceremony

and consideration for

some kind of final award.

In early summer I receive notice

of my retirement ceremony

in August at old Fort Meade.

I call the headquarters and find

that the First Army Band will play,

my first unit thirty years before.

I arrange to play the tuba with the same.

On a beautiful sunny August day,

with my family in the audience,

I march out from the reviewing stand

to join the band

and play a few final tunes

of military marching music

under the baton of another

retiring chief.

After I march back,

my wife stands at attention

next to me as the colonel

pins on the Meritorious Service Medal,

more deserved by those

who never returned from Nam

whose names line the wall on the Mall.

It is in their memory that this tribute

is dedicated; a memory never fading.

In addition to the dead,

the living junk of the war

was shipped back to the states

like the retrograde chassis

to be rebuilt in the depots

of VA hospitals and counseling centers,

often becoming homeless,

victims of drugs, alcohol, stress and Agent Orange.

Let them not become living dead,

The forgotten refuse of war.

19
Post-Retirement Postscript

A baker's dozen more years

pass with numerous milestones:

Parkinson's Disease and

kidney cancer

both requiring surgery,

neither on the VA list

of Official Agent Orange Diseases;

knee replacement surgery,

service-connected

but easier using

civilian insurance

in a local hospital

than going to a VA hospital.

The horrendous events of 911

remind me of Pearl Harbor,

which occurred when

I was in the womb.

"Remember Pearl Harbor"

was the motto of that Good War.

Likewise, "Remember 911"

seems to be justification

for the Afghan affair.

Iraq is another matter.

It feels like the Vietnam escalation,

followed by all of the

attendant problems

of occupying another country

while enduring

a low-tech insurgency

fought with AK-47s

RPGs and IEDs.

Twenty-first century techies

vs. WWII-era partisans.

Remember the V.C.

and their tire rubber sandals?

Add to that the religious factor-

with martyrs in the making

willing to take others with them.

Technological superiority alone

will never solve the

perennial problems

of incomplete intelligence,

collateral damage to civilians

or friendly fire incidents.

The Guard and Reserve,

a haven for draft dodgers

in my day,

is now overextended,

causing a call for the draft

possibly reversing the gains

of the volunteer military.

Continue to support

the troops and the vets,

especially those

who left limbs

on the field of battle,

remember those

lost their life in the struggle,

and pray for the seemingly impossible-

peace in our time.

VOLUME 3

MILLENNIAL MEDITATIONS

(POEMS, 2000-2003)

MEMORIES

Memories of Princeton

Princeton rises above

the coastal plains

of New Jersey

like a medieval fortress town

transplanted from Europe,

out of place in it's setting:

impressive on first sight;

quaint colonial history;

revolutionary war battlefield;

gothic spired university;

Georgian/Victorian seminary

(my abode long ago,

recently returned Viet vet

studying alongside

draft-dodging divinity students);

Institute of Advanced Studies

down the street

Einstein once walked

deep in profound thought,

with a burning pipe

in his jacket pocket

(so they say).

ED CALHOON

Home of:

world-class scholars,

some saints and/or geniuses,

but mostly

less-than-perfect people;

undergraduate students,

once big fish in little ponds

now floundering and gasping for air;

and graduate students,

perhaps amazed as I,

from a minor-league school,

making it to the Ivy League

awed by the fancy footwork

of academic all-stars.

I went away to try on

the robe and role of a cleric

finally withdrawing

in a classical calling crisis

feeling failure for not finishing.

Twenty years hence I returned,

first for reunion,

next year a seminar

on spiritual life

not taught in my student days.

I saw again the allure

of an academic oasis

nourishing parched minds;

also a new nurturing

of the Spirit's flame,

kept aglow through centuries

of dark nights of the soul.

My spiritual director Diogenes,

in name and fact

a philosopher,

taught timeless lessons

from the classics,

including catholic mystics.

He may eventually retire,

but such wisdom

is never retired,

1as it is passed on

to each generation

in the hallowed halls

of Princeton.

ED CALHOON

Millennial Musings

The turning of the year two thousand

Came and went amid quibbling

over whether it was really the millennium,

or just the last year of the last century,

not to mention biblical scholarship

which said Jesus was born

in three B.C.E.,

thus the apocalyptic milestone

had already passed uneventfully.

Nostradamus's prediction of disaster

in July of ninety-nine came to naught,

as did New Age warnings

of impending slippage

of the earth's crust

possibly to be triggered

by an errant asteroid

or other unheavenly body

firmly striking *terra firma*,

though such an event is always possible,

as witnessed the meteors hitting Jupiter.

Such scenarios make for

mediocre Made-For-TV Movies

or prophesy-fulfillment religious tracts

attempting to identify the Antichrist

(Bill Clinton or Bill Gates-

Bubba or Big Brother?).

Is Armageddon impending,

or are predictions of chaos

self-fulfilling given human nature?

Wars and rumors of wars,

like the poor, are always with us,

to paraphrase the Master.

Likewise earthquakes, winds and floods,

though we seem to make them worse,

through pollution and global warming,

followed by El Nino or La Nina, whatever.

Pestilence, real and virtual,

from AIDS and Ebola

to hackers' viruses and the over-hyped Y2K Bug.

ED CALHOON

This earth has been going to hell

since expulsion from the Heavenly Garden.

We long for the promised New Creation,

coincident with the Second Coming of Christ,

the First Coming of the Messiah

or the Next Reincarnation of The Buddha.

Will it be like the idealized future

of Buck Rogers, The Jetsons,

or any of the Star Trek generations?

With fantastic flying technology,

or a more down-to-earth

and gradually evolutionary changes?

What will the new millennium bring:

peace and prosperity finally, or more of the above?

Only whatever time is left will tell,

but an interesting time it will be.

MEDITATIONS

Who wants to be a millionaire?

The recently popular quiz show

raises the rhetorical question

"Who wants to be a millionaire?"

as if the answer is obvious:

everyone.

I beg to differ.

Recent history has shown

that winning a lottery

or a sweepstakes

is not the solution

to all one's problems,

and in fact creates more.

To those lessons, add

the eternal history

of inherited wealth

spent by prodigal sons,

not to mention

the Good Book's admonishment

about the love of money

ED CALHOON

being the source of evil.

Greed is one of the deadly sins,

in addition to the descriptive title

of the dreadful Fox rip-off show.

What I object to most,

as a meritocratic Jeopardy fan,

is the relative simplicity

of the questions

leading to such big prizes.

It is somewhat akin

to receiving a huge bequest

from a rich uncle

you never met.

You don't deserve it,

and as a result

squander it at the first opportunity.

Which is why puritans of old

and latter-day fundamentalists

often opposed lotteries

and games of chance.

Unlike Smith-Barney,

you didn't really earn it.

The same applies

to day-traders

and internet billionaires,

making their paper profits

on the whims of the market

or the timing of an IPO,

if not illegal insider trading.

The gods of chance giveth

and they taketh away.

The lessons of 1929

may have to be relearned:

millions can be lost

as fast as they were won.

My response to the question

asked above is: "not me";

and that is my final answer.

Shattering Shroud

Shattering the image

portrayed in pious pictures

of an other-worldly

spiritualized savior

suspended 'tween heaven and earth

as in Dali's painting:

replaced by a real man,

face distorted by torture,

congealed blood from his side,

scourge marks on his back,

thorn marks on his head,

nail marks on his wrists

(not his hands as on medieval

crucifixes and canvas);

heat-scorched photographic negative

with three-dimensional depth

touched up later with paint

and patched with newer linen

confusing carbon dating;

possibly preserved to provide

a skeptical scientist

or latter-day doubting Thomas

an astounding artifact—

a collapsed cocoon from

a fantastic flash-bang metamorphosis.

Easter Explosion

Something happened,

a biblical big bang,

it's effects like a shock wave

emanating from a singular event,

transforming scared fishermen

into dynamic leaders and martyrs

ready to die for

a messianic heir

to a defunct throne

in a country occupied

by the greatest power

of that age and place,

which put him

to a criminal's death

through torture and

public display

on a shameful scaffold,

making him

unclean carrion.

Hardly a mythical

god-king for the Gentiles

or a Davidic warrior-king

for his fellow Jews;

instead, an absurdity

to the former

and a stumbling block

to the latter.[2]

The shock wave extended

from Jerusalem to Judea, Samaria

and the ends of the earth,

per the ascension commission.[3]

The echo of that event

is heard again

and amplified anew

in each generation.

---

[2] cf. 1Corinthians 1:23
[3] cf. Acts 1:8

Christmas Quest

Literary criticism

was the Grinch

that stole Christmas,

as a result of an

incomplete seminary education.

The problem was not

disbelieving Santa and his elves,

but throwing out

the Baby Jesus

with the proverbial textual bathwater.

Scholars much smarter than me

(like the later Jesus Seminar)

were the source of my skepticism,

with their search, like Schweitzer,

in Quest of the Historical Jesus.

They try to pick out *pericopes,*

authentic nuggets of true text

mined from the ore of myth.

The danger is loosing faith

in the discarded slag heap of scripture.

After leaving seminary,

I wandered in the spiritual desert.

Then I read in "Roots"

about the author meeting a *griot*

in the African homeland of his ancestors.

He was a storyteller with

hundreds of years

of memorized narratives

encompassing the history

of his people.

He demonstrated the ability

of otherwise illiterate people

to accurately pass on

verbal traditions

through the centuries.

Later in my pilgrimage,

I read Cardinal Newman's *Apologia*,

ED CALHOON

in which he told of his

discovery of the continuity

of verbal and written tradition.

Tradition linked the apostles

and the early Church Fathers

leading to the Councils

that created the Canon of Scripture

and wrote the Creeds of the Church.

The living church and its message

created the Scripture,

not visa versa

(per the Protestant creed:

Sola Scriptura).

After becoming Catholic,

I completed the Spiritual Exercises

Of Saint Ignatius Loyola

using my limited imagination

to place myself in the Gospel stories.

My spiritual director was a Jesuit

Biblical scholar

who showed me it was possible

to do scriptural analysis

without discarding tradition.

He also showed an openness

to the new winds of the Spirit

blowing in the Charismatic movement,

which many other denominations

had been unable to accept and cast out.

I remembered a young sailor I met

In Vietnam who was one of

the first Catholic Charismatics

and was a beacon of light

in an otherwise dark situation.

I found that the Church

had adapted to the challenges

of each generation.

Saint Ignatius was part of

the Counter-Reformation.

ED CALHOON

Ignatius used many of the

terms of evangelical Protestantism

and even showed Charismatic gifts,

enough to be hauled before

the Inquisition under suspicion.

The Spirit that inspired the Scriptures

still speaks to the Church

in the new Millennium,

and as many Christmases

as are left to come.

HAIKU

Hero Haiku

The real heroes are

just doing their jobs and not

making any fuss.

Our childhood heroes:

Police, Fire Fighters, Soldiers;

taken for granted.

Uncommon valor

displayed by common people

under extreme stress.

Ordinary folks,

extraordinary acts:

selfless sacrifice.

What greater love than

giving your life for others

as was given you.

Haiku of Crime and Punishment
I. REVENGE

The oldest response

to evil and injury

is bloody revenge.

Ten or a hundred

or now many thousands of

lives taken for one.

Hands amputated

for petty thefts, and feet

for who knows what else.

Revenge is easy

to see in others, harder

to see in our self.

II. JUSTICE

Justice is a blind

goddess with scales balancing

crime and punishment.

An eye for an eye

is a step above revenge,

but can be brutal.

If pay-back in kind

is really impossible,

what are our options?

What is life and limb

worth in dollars or in years'

incarceration?

III. GRACE

Grace is defined as

an unmerited favor

(or undeserved gift.)

Forgiveness is the

form of grace hardest of all

for human nature.

We want to keep score

and have winners and losers,

other cheek unturned.

Like unprodigal

sons who resent their father's

gracious joyous gifts.

Apple Trees in Spring

Beautiful blossoms

Blooming in Spring renewal

Bring joy to my heart.

BIBLICAL VERSES

Violence Biblical and Modern

Hear this story of Samuel[4]

Not taught

In Sunday School

At least in my youth.

King Saul commanded

David to give him

One hundred Philistine foreskins

for the hand of his daughter Michal,

Either a kind of enforced bris

Or more like scalping

Done by American aborigines.

It was no more violent than

Biblical beheading or hacking

Bodies in many pieces,

Done in obedience to

The jealous God.

---

[4] Cf. I Samuel 18:25-27

ED CALHOON

However, we modern

Moralists prefer

High velocity bullets,

High explosives or special

Chemical, biological

and nuclear solutions

over dull blades.

It's quicker and more humane,

Like euthanizing animals

Rather than sacrificing them

On the altar of our God.

Two Biblical Women

Ruth is widely admired

for her loyalty and virtue

but by Naomi's instruction

she lay next to Boaz

on the threshing floor

after he had eaten and drunk

unto vulnerability.

She got her older rich man,

and lived happily

ever after,

becoming David's

great-Grandmother.[5]

Bathsheba is oft accused

of womanly wantonness,

where in fact the whole affair

was devised by David,

first as a voyeur

---

[5] Cf. Ruth 3:1-4:13

then as an abuser

of his powers as king

leading to murder by proxy.

Only Nathan's lamb parable

made David see

his own duplicity.[6]

---

[6] Cf. II Samuel 11:1-12:15

Solomon's Reign

For twenty years,

King Hiram of Tyre

Provided King Solomon

With cedar, cypress and gold

To build homes for himself and God.

In seeming gratitude,

Solomon gave Hiram

Twenty cities in Galilee.

Upon inspecting them,

Hiram declared them

"cabul' (good for nothing),

but still gave 120 talents

of gold in return.[7]

Solomon was fabled for his

Wisdom and diplomacy.

Why did he so disrespect

An old friend and ally?

Did he need the gold

To keep up his lifestyle?

---

[7]   Cf. I Kings 9:10-14

ED CALHOON

Maybe the people of Israel

got what they earlier asked of Samuel-

a real king with all the trimmings:

taxes, military draft and harem

with foreign wives and their idols.

Paper Power

By Edward J. Calhoon Sr., 2003

Ezra 5 and 6

Display the documents

Of ancient civil service,

And an amazingly modern

Willingness to fulfill

The promise of a previous king

return the treasures

of Solomon's temple

and allow its rebuilding.

The power of paperwork

In a rational system

Of administration

Is a wonder to behold,

notwithstanding

rampant red tape

And bungling bureaucracy.

Job's Lament

Job was a pawn

In a spiritual chess game

Between God and the Devil

To determine whether

Job was loyal

Only out of

Gratitude for gifts.

All of his riches

Were removed.

Job's friends tried

To blame the victim

Through a search

For unrepented sins.

Job longed

For the Good Old Days,

Days of milk and honey,

Like the first days

Of Israel in Caanan,

Or the days of youth

Seen from old age.

God asks rhetorical questions

From out of the whirlwind:

Is Job greater than

The greatest of God's creatures?;

The behemoth (elephant?)

On the land

Or leviathan (whale?)

In the sea?

In the whirlwind,

Job saw the Lord

As well as heard Him,

Finally convincing Job

Of his own lowliness.

Less convincing

Is the happy ending,

In which Job's fortunes

Are restored as before.

Once again, virtue is

Rewarded with riches.

Paul

Saul of Tarsus

was likely the

fruit of the womb

of a Jewish mother

from whom he inherited

his religion

and the son

of a gentile Roman father

from whom he inherited

his citizenship.

In his religious life

he was a zealous

Pharisee of the Pharisees

student of the

great rabbi Gamaliel

of Talmud fame.

Saul hunted down and

consented in the stoning

of Jewish Christians

like Stephen the deacon

first of many martyrs.

On the road to Damascus

he was knocked

to the ground

and blinded

by a light from heaven

Possibly lightning or epileptic fit?

Maybe it was the only way

God could get the attention

of a know-it-all rabbinical student.

From out of the darkness,

a voice spoke to him:

"Saul, Saul, why do you persecute me?"

"Who are you, Lord?" Saul asked.

"Jesus whom you are persecuting" he replied.

He "stood speechless",

probably for the first time in his life.

He became Paul, the unworthy

Apostle to the Gentiles.

He tried to be

all things to all people:

an observant Jew before Jews,

dividing the Jewish opposition

into warring factions

of Pharisees and Sadducees;

a Roman citizen by birth,

when it gave him status

before a judging local king,

allowing him to

appeal his case to Rome,

getting a free trip

to the center of civilization.

In his letter to the Romans,

Paul created a radical new theology:

justification by faith,

through God's grace

not the works of the Law.

He reckoned that circumcision

came after Abraham's faith

and the Law of Moses

was summarized by

a Law of Love.

Eating non-kosher food

or food sacrificed to idols

was now only a problem

if it caused others problems.

This is a far cry

from Daniel and his buddies

refusing to eat

the Babylonian king's

fine but non-kosher food

asking for veggies instead

and being cast into the oven.

Paul's Jewish-Christian opposition

is summed up by

James in his epistle:

"Show me your faith

apart from your works,

and I by my works

will show you my faith."

Jesus himself said

that he came

not to abolish

the Law and Prophets,

but to fulfill them.

He also said

ED CALHOON

we will be judged

by our actions

not just our words or beliefs:

the devils believe and tremble.

Bitter divisions came

from faith versus works

controversies through

the centuries and millennia,

first between Christians and Jews,

then between Protestants and Catholics.

Such quarrels are like the

chicken versus egg question-

unresolvable and unnecessary,

with the only explanation

a synthesis of the two

into a mystery (a good Catholic word).

Paul also accepted the norms

of the civilization around him

regarding women and slavery,

partly because of his belief

in the imminent Second Coming.

At his best, Paul said:

"There is neither Jew nor Greek,

... slave nor free,

... male nor female,

for you are one

in Christ Jesus."

Those words raise

a high ideal that

unfortunately was ignored

most of the intervening time,

while his statements

about not rocking the boat

with the status quo

were later used to justify

slavery and misogyny.

Despite his shortcomings,

Paul founded the Gentile

Christian churches

that survived underground

centuries until embraced

by an Emperor

ED CALHOON

and given the right to build

churches, cathedrals and basilicas

over burial grounds and catacombs

containing the bones

of the fathers of our faith,

such as saints Peter and Paul.

VISIONS

Serving the Other

Servanthood, suffering or otherwise,

has become almost incomprehensible.

Trusted old family servants no longer exist,

if they ever did in the dim past.

Servants are seen

as the modern equivalent of slaves,

and to paraphrase Lincoln,

nobody is volunteering for the job.

Mother Theresa,

serving the poorest of the poor,

was seen as an anachronism,

a throwback to an earlier age.

Service is as countercultural

as poverty and chastity,

in a culture that glorifies

money, sex and power.

Yet what is impossible to us

is possible to God,

and Jesus said

greatness requires service[8].

His greatness

was giving his life

as a ransom for us[9]:

let us give back in gratitude.

---

[8] Matthew 20:26
[9] Matthew 20:28

Goals

My goals are many—
accomplishments few;
judged wanting before
even starting.

My internal editor
shuts down the process
instead of allowing it
to flow freely.

The well of inspiration
is deep and hidden,
gushing forth
with cooling waters;

flowing from
the underground pool
of hidden feelings
often denied,

ED CALHOON

especially by men

whose left brain

dominates all thought

with logic not feeling.

Duplication is easy.

Creation is hard.

Reinventing the wheel is human.

Making the truly new is divine.

Disciple to Apostle

The followers of Jesus

the roaming rabbi

were fishermen first,

unlikely rabbinical students

with no synagogue to call classroom,

just the roads and fields

of gentile Galilee.

They had to progress

from students to teachers,

disciples to apostles,

denying cowards to preaching martyrs,

not through their own wisdom

but the power of God's Spirit.

In each generation

we need to develop disciples

and apostles will follow.

ED CALHOON

Post-911

Smoke rising

from stricken twin towers

then unimaginable collapse;

breach of walls

of seemingly impregnable

fortress of defense

in audacious offense

took my breath away

leading to grief,

gratitude for sacrifices

of everyday heroes

often unsung,

and anger at

lives cut short,

families devastated.

Tents

Tents were homes

to Semitic nomads

wandering through

Middle Eastern deserts.

They symbolize

commonality of community

among families and tribes

and welcoming of strangers.

Remember the prophet's peaceful vision

of God's Holy Mountain

where lion and lamb lie down

and swords become plowshares.

Imagine a tent encompassing

all kinds of Christians

covering ancient crevasses

from past divisions,

ED CALHOON

recognizing Catholic,

Orthodox, Evangelical

and Charismatic Christians

as parts of a Universal Church,

celebrating and sharing

the gifts brought by each

to the community

of faith in One Lord.

Imagine an even bigger tent

including all

spiritual children of Abraham,

serving the same God,

whom they call by

different names

such as Adonai, Allah or Abba

for a Divine Daddy/Mommy/Parent,

allowing us

to see each other

as brothers and sisters,

stop the killing,

relentless rounds

of revenge

oxymoronic holy wars,

and terrible terrorism,

canceling the

curse of Cain

that has plagued

all humankind.